CHESS TACTICS

for

BEGINNERS

CHESS TACTICS for BEGINNERS

By R. G. WADE,
RAYMOND BOTT,
STANLEY MORRISON

Edited by FRED REINFELD

Published by
Melvin Powers
WILSHIRE BOOK COMPANY
12015 Sherman Road
No. Hollywood, California 91605
Telephone: (213) 875-1711 / (818) 983-1105

STERLING CHESS BOOKS WRITTEN OR EDITED BY FRED REINFELD

Chess for Children
Chess Victory—Move by Move
Complete Book of Chess Openings
Complete Book of Chess Stratagems
Creative Chess
The Great Chess Masters and Their Games
How *Not* to Play Chess
How to Beat Your Opponent Quickly
1001 Brilliant Chess Sacrifices and Combinations
1001 Ways to Checkmate
Reinfeld Explains Chess

First Book of Chess (with co-author, I. A. Horowitz)
Second Book of Chess: The Nine Bad Moves
Third Book of Chess: How to Play the White Pieces
Fourth Book of Chess: How to Play the Black Pieces
Fifth Book of Chess: How to Win When You're Ahead
Sixth Book of Chess: How to Fight Back
Seventh Book of Chess: How to Play the King Pawn Openings
Eighth Book of Chess: How to Play the Queen Pawn Openings

ACKNOWLEDGMENT

To Chess Education Society, a society for fostering Chess within the educational system.

Copyright © 1961 by R. G. Wade, R. Bott, and S. Morrison
Published in the United States of America by Printed Arts Co., Inc.
Wilshire Book Company edition
is published by special arrangement with
Sterling Publishing Co., Inc.
Manufactured in the United States of America
Library of Congress Catalog Card No.: 61-10395

ISBN 0-87980-019-4

CONTENTS

CHESS NOTATION

As indicated in the following diagram, all the squares on the chessboard are *numbered* from both sides of the board; White's KR1, for example, is Black's KR8. Each square is also *named* for the piece occupying the file. Below the diagram is a list of the chief abbreviations used in chess notation.

BLACK

QR8	QN8	QB8	Q8	K8	KB8	KN8	KR8
QR7	QN7	QB7	Q7	K7	KB7	KN7	KR7
QR6	QN6	QB6	Q6	K6	KB6	KN6	KR6
QR5	QN5	QB5	Q5	K5	KB5	KN5	KR5
QR4	QN4	QB4	Q4	K4	KB4	KN4	KR4
QR3	QN3	QB3	Q3	K3	KB3	KN3	KR3
QR2	QN2	QB2	Q2	K2	KB2	KN2	KR2
QR1	QN1	QB1	Q1	K1	KB1	KN1	KR1

WHITE

King — K		check — ch	
Queen — Q		discovered check — dis ch	
Rook — R		double check — dbl ch	
Bishop — B		en passant — e.p.	
Knight — N		good move — !	
Pawn — P		very good move — ! !	
captures — x		outstanding move — ! ! !	
to — —		bad move — ?	
at — /		becomes Queen — /	

6

VALUES OF THE CHESSMEN

The following table of values is accepted as standard:

Queen	♛	9 points
Rook	♜	5 points
Bishop	♝	3 points
Knight	♞	3 points
Pawn	♟	1 point

In actual practice, most games are decided by superiority of force. For this reason, it is essential to maintain equality of material.

The value of this table is at once apparent. It shows, for example, that you can readily give up a Knight to get a Bishop in return (or vice versa). To give up the Queen for a Pawn would, however, be idiotic, unless a very important return (such as checkmate) were immediately available.

Similarly, to give up a Rook for a Bishop would not be good, unless one picked up several Pawns to make the transaction a fairly even one.

INTRODUCTION

Recently a friend of mine was telling me of the great enjoyment his 12-year-old son gets from chess. "The only thing that bothers me, though," he added, "is that he seems to lack any aggressive winning ideas. He's satisfied to play from move to move and doesn't even mind being on the defensive. The timidity of his chess play is certainly not in keeping with his character."

This timidity is of course characteristic of many inexperienced young players—and not only young players. True, they get a great deal of enjoyment out of chess, but they could get so much more if they knew how to play to win—how to play aggressively—how to exploit their opponent's mistakes, how to attack, threaten, set traps. Once a player has grasped these fascinating winning methods his pleasure in chess increases a thousandfold and so does his playing ability.

This is the realization on which the following book is based. We have here a unique combination of authors who understand chess and who are also highly skilled devoted teachers. The result is a book which is exceptionally clear, very easy to follow and enormously useful in conveying the essence of CHESS TACTICS.

—*Fred Reinfeld*

I. THE KNIGHT FORK

Basic Patterns

Example No. I—Black to move

White's Knight checks the Black King while forking Black's King and Queen.

As Black must move his King out of check, he has no time to save his Queen.

White therefore wins the Black Queen.

Example No. 2—White to move

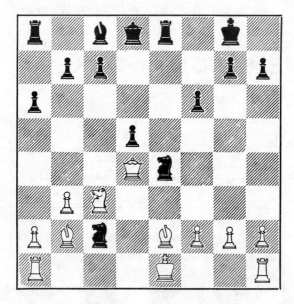

Black's advanced Knight is giving check and forking White's Queen and Queen Rook at the same time. Such a triple attack is jokingly called a "family check" or "family fork."

White must move his King out of check.

He therefore has no time to save his menaced Queen or Rook.

Puzzle No. 1—White to move

White has a Knight fork which will result in a decisive gain of material for him.

How does White proceed?

(See solutions in back of book.)

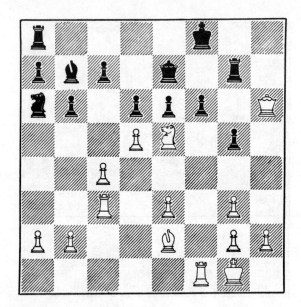

Puzzle No. 2—White to move

White has an obvious and good move in 1 R × P ch. But this is not the very best, as he has a crushing Knight fork at his disposal.

What is the right move, and why is Black defenceless against it?

Puzzle No. 3—White to move

If White starts off with the right forcing move, he can bring about a position in which a Knight fork will win Black's Rook for the Knight. What is the sequence that White needs?

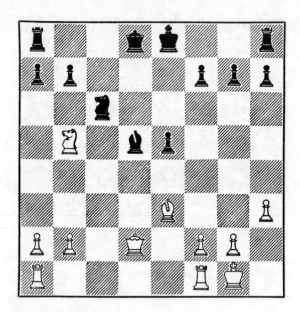

Puzzle No. 4—White to move

White can win a piece by a startling capture followed by a Knight fork. How should White begin, and what is the Knight fork with which he will follow up?

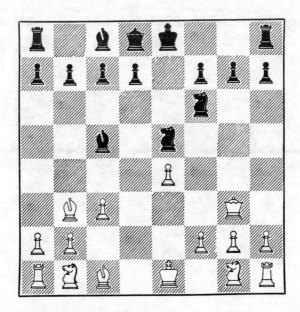

Puzzle No. 5—Black to move

Black can force White to move his King or Queen. Whichever one of these pieces moves, Black then continues with a crushing Knight fork.

What is the sequence which Black can force? What Knight fork would follow White's King move? What Knight fork would follow White's Queen move?

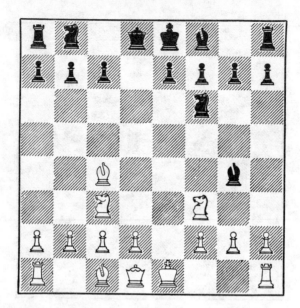

Puzzle No. 6—White to move

What move does White need in order to lead up to a profitable Knight fork? Give White's first move, Black's reply, and White's second move.

Puzzle No. 7—White to move

White prepares a Knight fork with an astonishing preliminary move, winning a Pawn in the process.

What are the moves making up this sequence?

(This line of play was overlooked by a World Champion!)

Puzzle No. 8—White to move

By threatening mate White sets the stage for a Knight fork that leaves him a clear piece ahead. How does play proceed?

2. THE PIN

Basic Patterns

Example No. 3

A piece is said to be pinned when it is attacked along a line from which it cannot move without exposing a second piece (the "screened piece") to capture.

In the case of an absolute pin (where the King is the screened piece) the pinned piece cannot legally move.

In the case of a relative pin, the screened piece can legally move, although as a rule this is undesirable because it would lose material.

In the above diagram the White Queen is pinned by the Black Rook. This is an absolute pin as the Queen screens the White King from attack.

Example No. 4

Here the Black Knight is pinned by the White Bishop. If the Knight moves, White replies B × Q.

Puzzle No. 9—White to move

The Black King and Queen are on the same diagonal. How can White take advantage of the situation by means of a deadly pin?

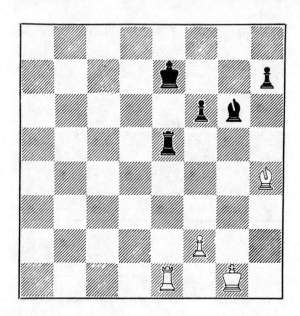

Puzzle No. 10—White to move

Black's King Bishop Pawn is tied to the diagonal by White's Bishop. How can White take advantage of this?

Puzzle No. 11—Black to move

White's Queen Pawn is pinned, in the sense that it cannot make a capture without exposing the White Queen to capture. How can Black take advantage of this?

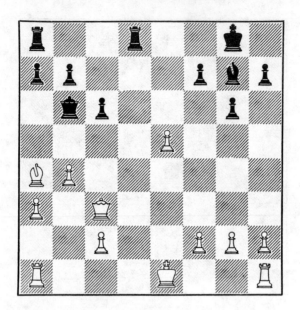

Puzzle No. 12—Black to move

Is White's King Pawn properly protected? If your answer is "No", how would you prove your claim?

Puzzle No. 13—White to move

For the moment Black's Queen is pinned on a diagonal. It is therefore unable to carry out its function of guarding the Black Rook.

White takes advantage of this in a very surprising but thoroughly logical manner. How?

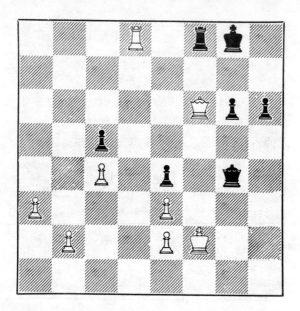

Puzzle No. 14—Black to move

White's Queen is pinned by Black's Rook, but this piece is pinned in turn by White's Rook.

Does Black have to play.., R×R, or does he have something better?

Puzzle No. 15—White to move

Black's Bishop Pawn is pinned on the diagonal. Black's Rook, which attacks White's Queen, is itself pinned, as it cannot expose the Black Queen to attack by moving horizontally.

How can White benefit from these two pins?

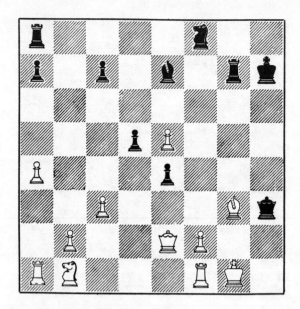

Puzzle No. 16—Black to move

White's Bishop is pinned by a Black Rook and also attacked by the Black Queen. As matters stand, however, the Bishop is adequately guarded by White's King Bishop Pawn.

How can Black undermine this protection?

3. THE SKEWER

Basic Patterns

Example No. 5—Black to move

A skewer is an attack on two pieces on the same line, which has the effect of compelling the piece nearest the attacker to move, leaving the other piece to be taken.

Here the Black King and Queen are in line on a file. The White Rook gives check, forcing the Black King to move. This results in the loss of the Black Queen.

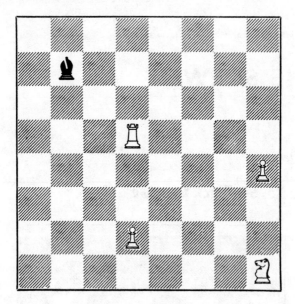

In this position the Black Bishop is skewering the White Rook and Knight on the long diagonal. Any Rook move will expose the Knight to capture.

Puzzle No. 17—White to move

Black's King and Queen are on the same diagonal. Does this suggest a possible skewer attack to you?

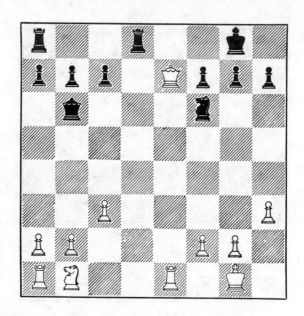

Puzzle No. 18—Black to move

Where would you look for a skewer?

Having determined White's vulnerable line, how would you proceed?

Puzzle No. 19—White to move

Black threatens to play . . , R—R1 mate.

However, it is White's move, and if he finds the best line he can force the Black King and Rook into a skewer.

Demonstrate White's winning procedure.

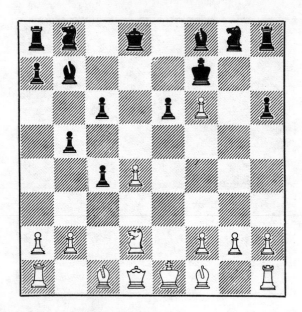

Puzzle No. 20—White to move

White has a move which will force two Black pieces in line for a winning skewer.

Give White's next two moves.

Puzzle No. 21—White to move

Black's King and Queen are on the same diagonal.

At the moment the skewer Q—KB3 ch does not work, as Black can reply . . , K × Q.

However, with proper play White *can* exploit the vulnerable position of the Black King and Queen.

How does White build up a winning skewer attack?

Puzzle No. 22—White to move

Black's King and Queen are in line for a skewer, but the Black Queen Pawn blocks the all-important line.

How can White force the line open in order to carry out the skewer attack?

Puzzle No. 23—Black to move

Is it necessary for Black to defend his Pawn?
What is Black's strongest move?
What does it threaten?
What can White do about it?

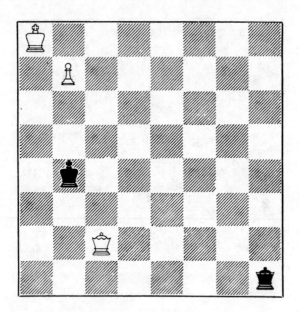

Puzzle No. 24—White to move

Black's Queen pins the White Pawn and thereby prevents its advance to the queening square.

What finesse must White adopt to force the queening of the Pawn?

4. MORE FORKS

Basic Patterns

Example No. 7

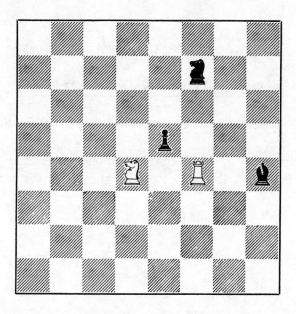

In Chapter 1 you saw that a Knight fork is an attack on two or more hostile pieces at the same time. Other pieces also have this power to attack simultaneously in different directions.

In the above diagram, for example, the Black Pawn is forking the White Knight and the White Rook. The White Rook is forking Black's Knight and Bishop.

Example No. 8

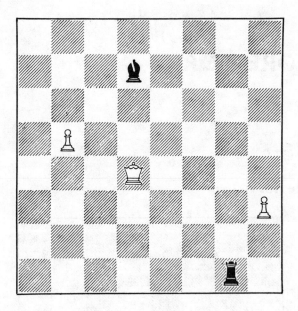

White's Queen attacks the Black Rook *and* the Black Bishop at the same time.

Our impression of the Queen's enormous power is heightened by the fact that.., R—N2 (to protect the Bishop) is out of the question.

Black's Bishop forks the two White Pawns.

Puzzle No. 25—White to move

Find a move that forks the Black King and Rook.

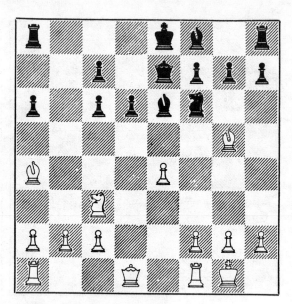

Puzzle No. 26—White to move

White has a fork that wins a Rook.

Puzzle No. 27—White to move

White makes an attacking move that sets up a position for a Pawn fork.

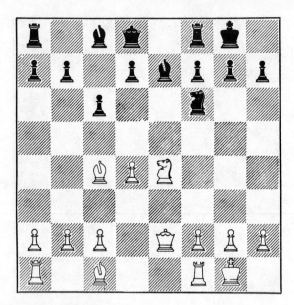

Puzzle No. 28—Black to move

With the proper preparation, Black can win a piece by means of a Pawn fork.

Puzzle No. 29—White to move

White forces the Bishop to move to a square on which it will be the victim of a fork.

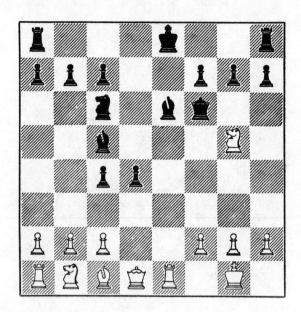

Puzzle No. 30—White to move

How should White proceed to set up a winning fork?

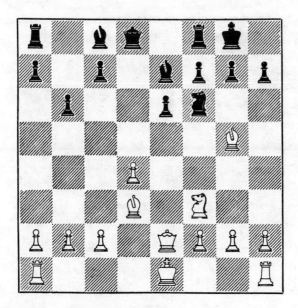

Puzzle No. 31—White to move

The fact that Black's Queen Rook is unprotected gives White the opportunity for a winning fork. How?

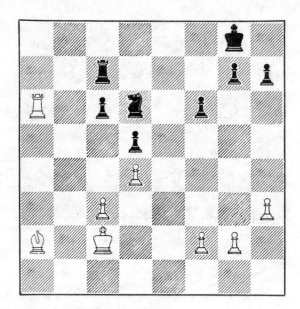

Puzzle No. 32—White to move

Despite the apparent solidity of Black's position, White can break through violently in order to prepare a winning fork. What are the two moves he needs for this purpose?

5. DISCOVERED CHECK

A discovered check occurs when a move by one piece *uncovers* check by another piece.

The checking piece will be a Bishop, Rook, or Queen.

Basic Patterns

Example No. 9a—White to move

Any move of the White Bishop produces a discovered check by the White Rook.

Example No. 9b—Black to move

White's Bishop has moved, enabling the White Rook to give discovered check.

Example No. 10a—White to move

Any move of White's Bishop will produce a discovered check by White's Rook. The strongest discovered check is the capture of Black's Knight.

Example No. 10b—Black to move

White's Bishop has captured the Black Knight. Black is unable to reply .., P × B because the Bishop capture has created a discovered check by White's Rook. Thus the discovered check has enabled White to win a piece.

Puzzle No. 33—White to move

The White Knight stands between the White Rook and the Black King. Consequently any move of the Knight will produce a discovered check. Which Knight move is the strongest?

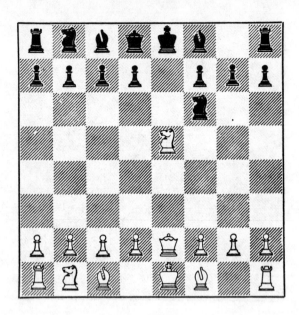

Puzzle No. 34—White to move

White has eight possible discovered checks by moving his Knight from King 5. Which is the strongest discovered check?

Puzzle No. 35—Black to move

Black's King is in check. Does this mean that Black must move his King out of check ? Or does Black have some more advantageous reply ?

Puzzle No. 36—Black to move

Black would like to advance his King Pawn, giving discovered check with his Bishop. However, the White Queen prevents this. What can Black do about it?

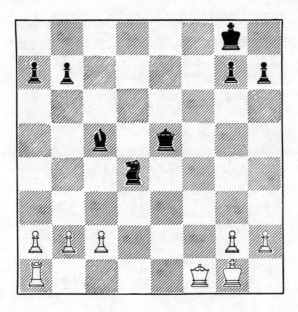

Puzzle No. 37—Black to move

Black has a number of possible discovered checks.

Two of these, in fact, are "double" checks. A double check—
two pieces checking at the same time—is actually a form of discovered check. There is only one way of answering a double check
—by moving the King.

What would be the consequences of the double checks in this
case?

Puzzle No. 38—White to move

How can White win a great deal of material by a series of discovered checks?

Puzzle No. 39—White to move

If White plays the right first move, he can achieve one of the following objectives: (a) win a piece or (b) entice Black's King into a devastating discovered check.

What is White's proper continuation?

Note in the above diagram that all the White forces are in Black's sector and all the Black forces are in White's sector.

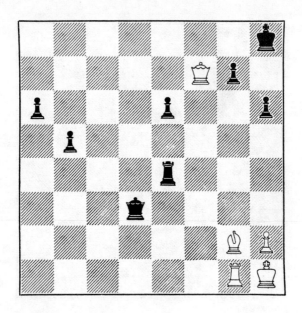

Puzzle No. 40—White to move

The obvious move 1 B×R allows Black to draw with 1 .., Q×B ch, as White has no escape from the resulting perpetual checks by the Queen.

However, White has an alternative procedure which wins for him. What is this alternative procedure?

THERE IS SOMETHING EVEN BETER HERE!

1 QB8 + , KR2
2 BXR + ,   WGLL?

3 QXP XXNG

6. REMOVING THE GUARD

(i) *Destroying the guard*

Basic Pattern

Example No. 11—Black to move

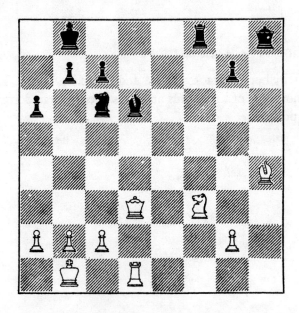

    White's Knight has the function of guarding his Bishop. Black removes the guardian Knight with 1.., R × N. After White captures the Rook Black replies 2.., Q × B, having obtained the material advantage of two minor pieces for a Rook.

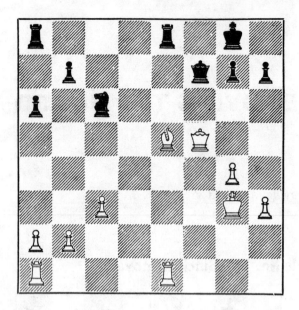

Puzzle No. 41—Black to move

White's Bishop is attacked twice and defended twice. How can Black remove one of the guards and thus decisively undermine the Bishop's position?

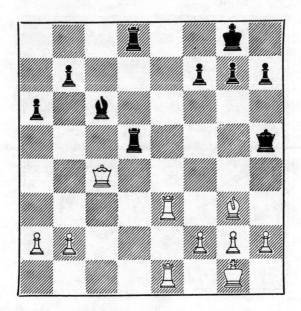

Puzzle No. 42—White to move

Black has to guard his back row against the potential mating threat R—K8 ch etc. If White is alive to the possibilities he can win material by removing one of the guards.

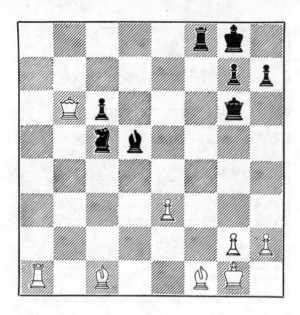

Puzzle No. 43—Black to move

White's Bishop at King Bishop 1 has the vital function of preventing.., Q×P mate. How then should Black proceed?

(ii) *Luring the guard away*

Basic Pattern

Example No. 12—Black to move

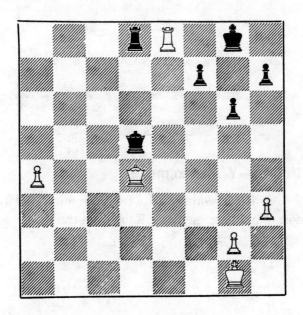

Black's Rook has the task of defending his Queen.

However, having played R—K8 ch, White forces the Black Rook to move from the guarded square. Black must play.., R × R losing his Queen.

Puzzle No. 44—White to move

Black's Rook is preventing White from queening his Pawn.
How does White lure the Black Rook from the King Rook file?

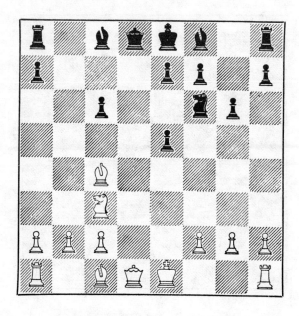

Puzzle No. 45—White to move

Find which Black pieces are attacked and examine how they are defended. One of the Black pieces can be deflected from a key defensive task. How?

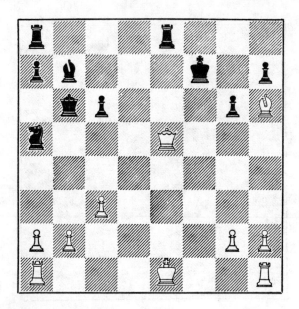

Puzzle No. 46—White to move

It would seem that White's Queen is lost because it is pinned by a Black Rook on the King file.

Yet White can upset the pin by luring the Black Rook from the critical file. How is this prepared and accomplished?

(iii) *Overworked pieces*

Basic Pattern

Example No. 13—Black to move

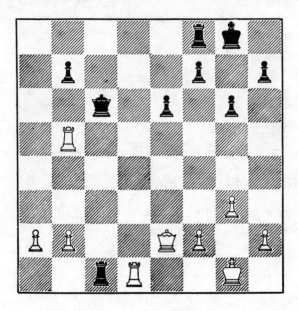

White's Queen has the job of defending both White Rooks. One of these Rooks is attacked by a Black Rook; the other White Rook is attacked by the Black Queen.

It follows that if one of the White Rooks is captured, the White Queen in the course of recapturing cannot continue to defend the remaining White Rook.

The play: Black starts with 1 .., R × R ch. White must reply 2 Q × R, giving up the protection of the other Rook. Black follows up with 2 .., Q × R with a Rook to the good.

White's Queen was an overworked piece.

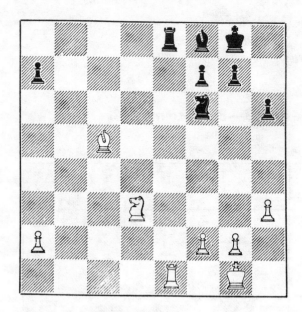

Puzzle No. 47—Black to move

Show that one of White's pieces is overworked, and how Black can turn this to his own advantage.

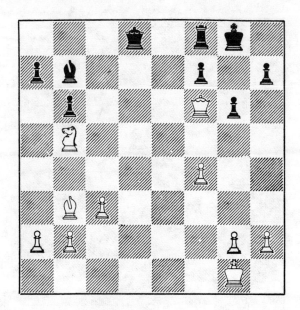

Puzzle No. 48—White to move

Black's overworked Rook has the double task of defending the Black Queen and the doubly-attacked Black Bishop Pawn as well. Show how this makes it possible to gain material decisively.

Puzzle No. 49—White to move

In trying to stop one of the White Pawns from queening, the Black pieces become overworked. How does White win?

7. ROOK CHECKMATES

Basic Patterns

Example No. 14

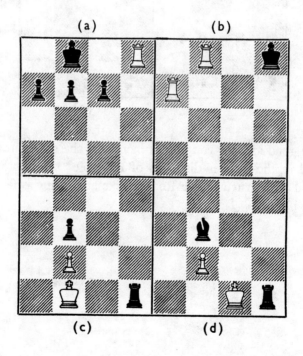

(a)　　　　　　(b)

(c)　　　　　　(d)

The mates pictured in the quarter-diagrams of Examples 14 and 15 are types that occur very often in practical play.

Example No. 15

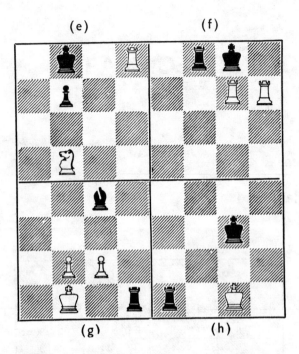

(e) (f)

(g) (h)

It is a good idea for you to set up on your chessboard the mates pictured in the quarter diagrams of Examples 14 and 15. Then see if you can construct other Rook checkmates, using as few chessmen as possible.

Puzzle No. 50—White to move

White forces mate in two moves. This is a good example of the power of the co-operating Rooks.

Puzzle No. 51—Black to move

Black mates in two moves. The first of these two moves is a "quiet" waiting and limiting move. This unpretentious-looking move forces the White King into a mating situation.

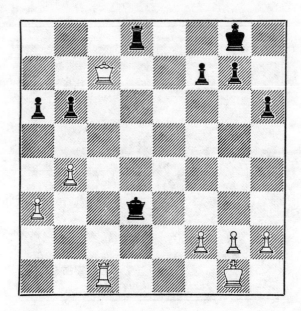

Puzzle No. 52—Black to move

Black forces mate in two moves on the back row. He starts with a sacrifice.

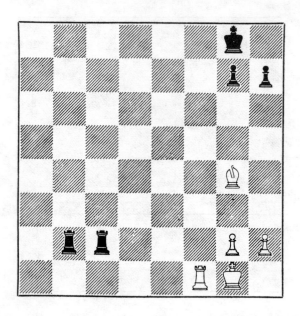

Puzzle No. 53—White to move

White forces mate in two moves.

If it were Black's turn to play in the above diagram, he could force mate in three moves. How?

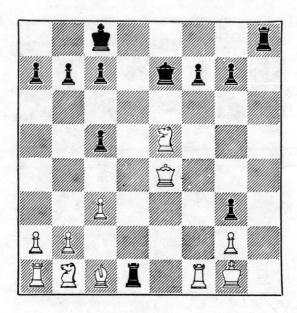

Puzzle No. 54—Black to move

Black forces mate in two moves.

Hint: Black's advanced Pawn at King Knight 6 confines White's King to the back row.

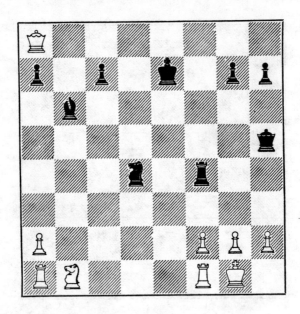

Puzzle No. 55—Black to move

Black forces mate in three moves.
Hint: study the quarter-diagram of Example No. 15 (e).

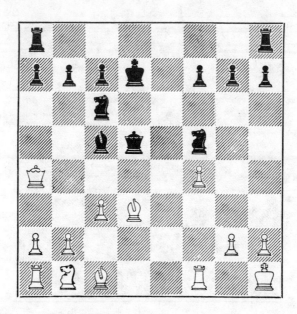

Puzzle No. 56—Black to move

Black forces mate in two moves.

Hint: study the quarter-diagram of Example No. 15 (g). There is a resemblance between the two positions which should become clear to you after careful study.

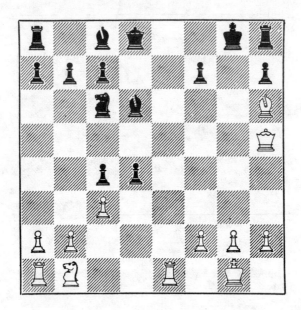

Puzzle No. 57—White to move

Although Black's Queen guards the back row, White forces mate in three moves by taking advantage of the fact that the Black Queen is overworked. How?

8. BISHOP CHECKMATES

Basic Patterns

Example No. 16

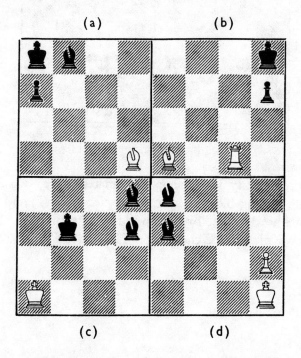

The quarter-diagrams illustrate various types of Bishop checkmates. In (a) a Bishop mates unassisted. In (b) a Bishop with the aid of a Rook—a very common pattern. In (c) and (d) two Bishops checkmate a cornered King.

Example No. 17

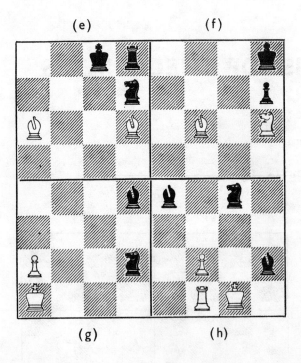

(g)   (h)

Here are more typical Bishop checkmates. In (e) two Bishops checkmate a King blocked by its own pieces. In (f) and (g) the checkmates are delivered by Bishop and Knight. In (h) two Bishops aided by a Knight force checkmate. This too is a rather common pattern.

84

SHORT GAMES

The two following brief games illustrate checkmating patterns with the Bishop.

WHITE	BLACK
1 P—K4	P—K4
2 N—QB3	N—KB3
3 B—B4	N×P
4 N—B3	N×N
5 QP×N	P—Q3

White has sacrificed a Pawn in order to develop his pieces on open lines.

| 6 Castles | B—N5 ? |
| 7 N×P! | .... |

This looks like a blunder. It isn't.

7	B×Q
8 B×P ch	K—K2
9 B—N5 mate	

WHITE	BLACK
1 P—Q4	P—KB4
2 B—N5	P—KR3
3 B—R4	P—KN4
4 B—N3	P—B5

In his single-minded determination to trap the Bishop, Black forgets that he is endangering his King.

| 5 P—K3! | .... |

As the Queen can move like a Bishop, it can also checkmate like a Bishop. Here the threat is 6 Q—R5 mate.

| 5 .... | P—KR4 |

OR N B3 ?

| 6 B—Q3 | .... |

This time White threatens 7 B—N6 mate.

| 6 .... | R—R3 ? |

N–R3 ? – Q×P !

This Rook turns out to be overworked.

7 Q×P ch!   ....

A pretty sacrifice to lure away the Black Rook.

  7 ....   R×Q

  8 B—N6 mate

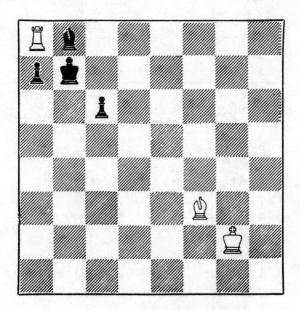

Puzzle No. 58—Black to move

Can Black safely capture the White Rook?

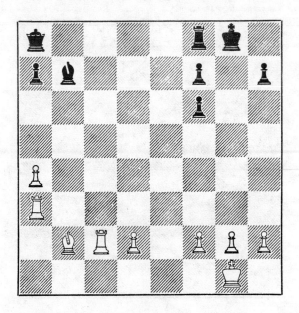

Puzzle No. 59—White to move

White forces mate in two moves. How?

Puzzle No. 60—White to move

White forces mate in three moves.
Note how smoothly the Bishops co-operate.

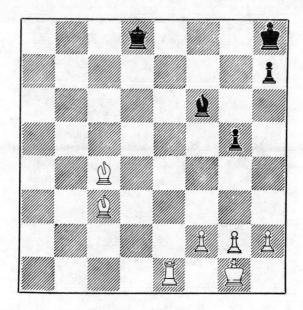

Puzzle No. 61—White to move

White can either checkmate in two moves or force Black to give up his Queen for a Bishop to avoid the mate.

White's technique is to deflect the Black Queen.

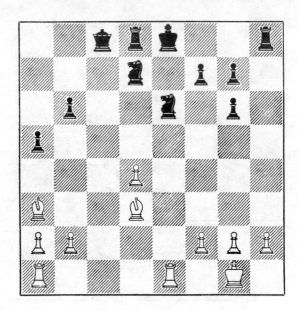

Puzzle No. 62—White to move

How many moves does White need to force mate?
Hint: see the quarter-diagrams (e) of Example No. 17.

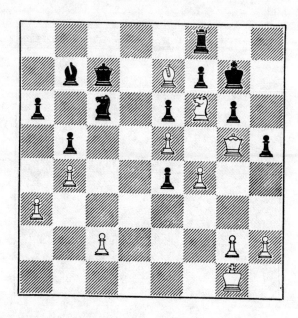

Puzzle No. 63—White to move

White forces mate in two moves.

Hint: Study quarter-diagram (f) of Example No. 17 and turn it onto its side!

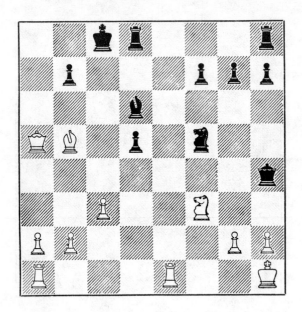

Puzzle No. 64—Black to move

Black forces mate in four moves.

Hint: the procedure is similar to that of Puzzle No. 63—but more complicated.

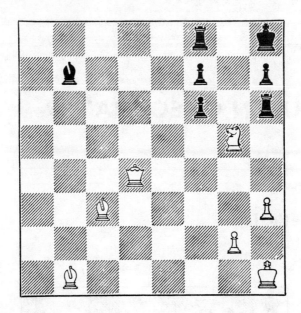

Puzzle No. 65—White to move

White forces mate in three moves.
Hint: study quarter-diagram (h) of Example No. 17.

9. QUEEN CHECKMATES

Basic Patterns

Example No. 18

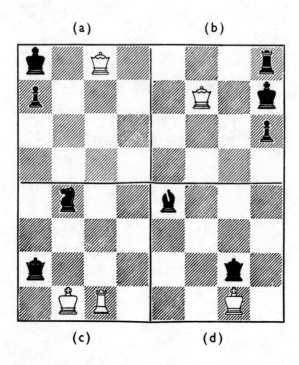

The Queen moves like a Rook or Bishop and can mate like either one of these pieces. The Queen is often supported by another piece in mating attacks.

Example No. 19

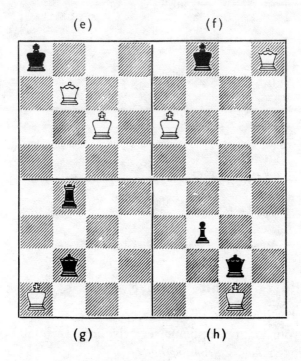

(e)   (f)

(g)   (h)

The Queen moves, and may mate, like a Rook and Bishop combined. The Queen is often supported by another piece in mating attacks.

Set up these patterns on your chessboard. See how many similar checkmate positions you can construct.

Puzzle No. 66—White to move

White forces mate in two moves.

Hint: your first move should severely limit the mobility of the Black King *without stalemating him !*

Puzzle No. 67—White to move

White forces mate in four moves, each of the moves being a check.

Don't let the Black King escape!

Hint: the mating process hinges on an all-important discovered check.

Puzzle No. 68—White to move

White forces mate in two moves.

Hint: White's first move cuts down the mobility of the Black King and forces him to approach the White King.

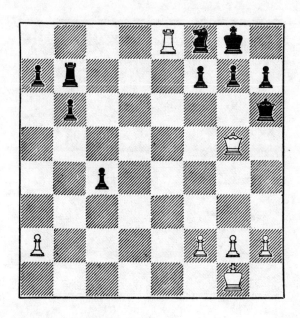

Puzzle No. 69—White to move

White forces mate in two moves.
Hint: see quarter-diagram (a) of Example No. 18.

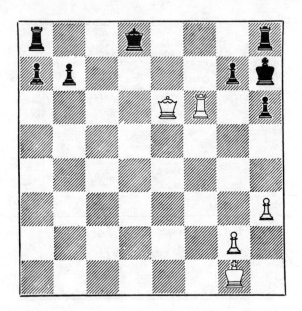

Puzzle No. 70—White to move

White forces mate in two moves.

Hint: the end-position is similar to that of quarter-diagram (b) of Example No. 18.

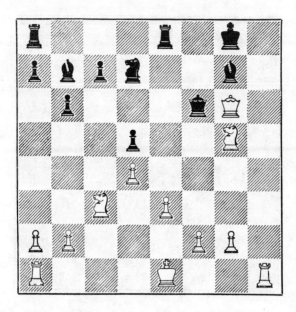

Puzzle No. 71—White to move

White forces mate in two moves.

Note that 1 Q—R7 ch will not do at all, as it allows the Black King to escape.

Instead, you need a preparatory move that stops the flight and makes mate possible on the following move.

Puzzle No. 72—White to move

White's Bishop at King 3 stands in the way of his immediately forcing checkmate.

However, White can force checkmate in two moves. How?

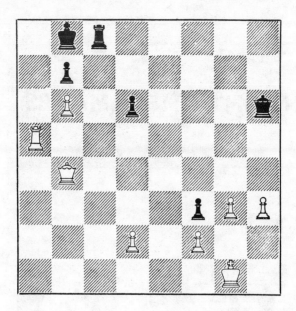

Puzzle No. 73

If White moves first in this curious position, he can force checkmate in three moves.

On the other hand, if Black moves first, he can force checkmate in four moves.

Demonstrate both checkmates.

10. KNIGHT CHECKMATES

Basic Patterns

Example No. 20

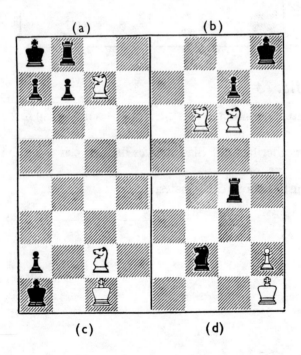

These are some typical patterns for Knight checkmates. In quarter-diagram (a) we have the smothered mate—King trapped by its own pieces—also known as Philidor's Legacy.

Example No. 21

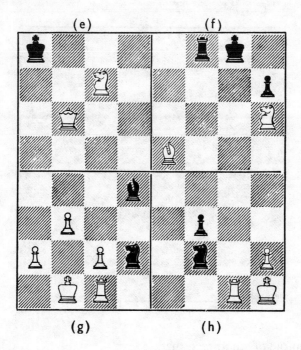

(e)   (f)

(g)   (h)

More Knight checkmates. Note that in all these typical cases the mated King is in the corner or near it.

Example No. 22—White to move

An example of smothered mate:

    1 Q—N8 ch!   R×Q
    2 N—B7 mate

SHORT GAME

The following little game shows a case of smothered mate in over-the-board play.

	WHITE	BLACK
1	P—K4	P—QB3
2	P—Q4	P—Q4
3	N—QB3	P×P
4	N×P	N—Q2
5	Q—K2	KN—B3??

He overlooks White's threat.

6 N—Q6 mate

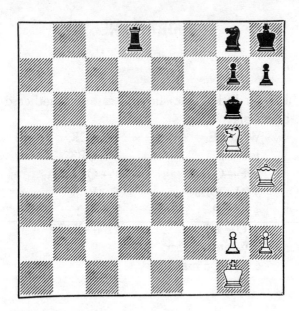

Puzzle No. 74—White to move

As matters stand, Black's Queen prevents White from executing a smothered mate.

Find a move that enables White to force mate in two moves.

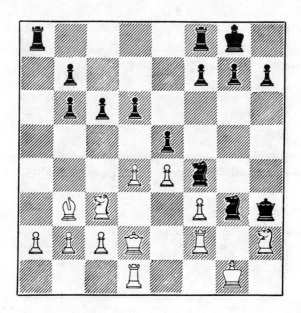

Puzzle No. 75—Black to move

Black can force mate in two moves.
Hint: see quarter-diagram (b) of Example No. 20.

Puzzle No. 76—White to move

White forces mate in two moves. How?

Hint: see quarter-diagram (c) of Example No. 20.

Puzzle No. 77—Black to move

Black can force mate in two moves. How?

Hint: a White Rook prevents a Knight checkmate by Black. Can this Rook be deflected from its station?

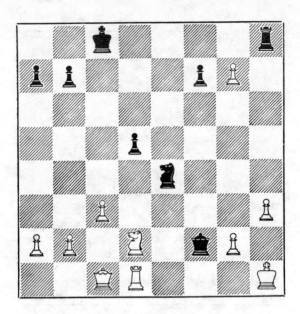

Puzzle No. 78—Black to move

Black can force mate in two moves. How?
Hint: see quarter-diagram (e) of Example No. 21.

Puzzle No. 79—White to move

White forces mate in two moves. How?
Hint: see quarter-diagram (f) of Example No. 21.

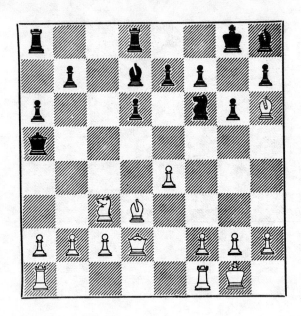

Puzzle No. 80—White to move

White has a move which ensures a substantial gain of material by threatening mate. What is the move?

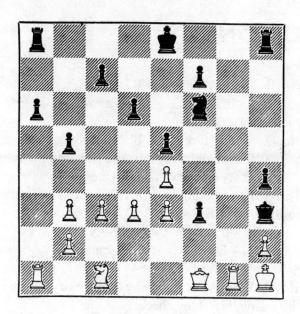

Puzzle No. 81—Black to move

Black has a move that threatens mate and results in a decisive gain of material. What is the move?

SOLUTIONS

Puzzle No. 1 By playing 1 N—K7 ch White forks the Black King and Queen. Black's King must move, allowing White to continue with 2 N × Q.

Puzzle No. 2 White forks the Black King and Queen with 1 N—N6 ch. Black is helpless against the Knight fork, as his Rook on King Knight 2 is *pinned* by White's Queen.

Puzzle No. 3 By checking with his Bishop, White sets up the desired position for a Knight fork:

1 B—B3 ch	K—N1
2 N—B6 ch	K moves
3 N × R and wins	

Puzzle No. 4 White wins a piece by a temporary Queen sacrifice followed by a Knight forking check:

1 Q × B!	Q × Q
2 N—B7 ch	K moves
3 N × Q and wins	

Puzzle No. 5 Black's winning move is 1 .., B × P ch! attacking White's King and Queen. Whichever way White captures the Bishop, he loses his Queen to a Knight fork.

For example, if White plays 2 K × B, Black replies 2.., N × P ch —a Knight fork that wins the White Queen.

Of if White plays 2 Q × B, Black replies 2.., N—Q6 ch— another Knight fork still winning the White Queen.

Puzzle No. 6 White plays 1 B × P ch!

If Black replies 1.., K—Q2, White plays 2 N—K5 ch forking King and Bishop. He continues 3 N × B which leaves him a piece ahead.

If Black replies 1.., K × B, White likewise plays 2 N—K5 ch (another Knight fork) and 3 N × B with a Pawn ahead and a highly advantageous position.

Puzzle No. 7 White's astonishing preliminary move is 1 Q—R8 ch! to which Black must of course reply 1.., K×Q. Now White has 2 N×P ch (forking the Black King and Queen) followed by 3 N×Q. With two Pawns to the good, White will have little trouble winning.

Puzzle No. 8 1 N—B6! ....

This threatens 2 R—R7 mate or 2 R—N8 mate. Black's Pawn at Queen 2 is pinned: if he plays 1.., P×N White replies 2 R×Q winning easily.

        1 ....   K×R

But now White has a Knight forking check which wins the Black Queen.

        2 N—Q8 ch   K moves
        3 N×Q and wins

White's victory is slow but sure. Sooner or later he will win all the Black Pawns and then he will queen his remaining Pawn.

Puzzle No. 9 With 1 B—B4 White attacks the Black Queen. Screening the Black King from attack on the diagonal, the Black Queen is lost.

Puzzle No. 10 Black's King Bishop Pawn, being pinned on the diagonal, does not really protect the Black Rook. White wins by 1 R×R ch, as Black cannot retake.

Puzzle No. 11 Black wins a piece with 1.., Q×B as White's Queen Pawn is pinned. After 2 P×Q Black replies 2.., R×Q.

Puzzle No. 12 White's King Pawn is not adequately protected as Black proves by playing 1.., B×P! This leaves White a sad choice between two unsatisfactory courses.

One is to play 2 Q×B, whereupon Black plays 2.., R—K1 pinning the White Queen on the King file, so that the Queen is lost.

The second unsatisfactory course is for White to move his Queen off the diagonal (instead of 2 Q×B). But then Black plays 2.., B×R winning easily.

Puzzle No. 13 White exploits the pin on Black's Queen with the surprising move 1 R—Q1. Being pinned, Black's Queen cannot capture the White Rook. There follows:

      1 ....   Q×Q

Now if White replies 2 P × Q ? ?, Black plays 2.., R × R ch with a Rook ahead. Instead of losing a Rook, however, White wins a Rook.

      2 R × R ch   K moves
      3 P × Q and wins

White is a Rook ahead.

Puzzle No. 14 Black exploits the pin on White's Queen with 1.., Q—R5 ch. This wins White's Queen.

Puzzle No. 15 White makes use of the double pin to play 1 R—Q5 ch! In that case Black cannot play 1.., P × R because of the pin on his Bishop Pawn.

So Black has the sorry choice between (a) moving his King and losing his Rook or (b) playing 1.., R × R, allowing White to reply 2 Q × Q.

Puzzle No. 16 Black undermines the protection of White's Bishop by playing 1.., B—B4.

This pins White's King Bishop Pawn and leaves White defenceless against the coming .., R × B mate.

Puzzle No. 17 With Black's King and Queen on the same diagonal, White wins the Queen with the skewer attack 1 B—N5 ch.

Puzzle No. 18 With White's Queen and King Rook lined up on the same file, we look for a skewer on the King file. The desired move is 1.., R—K1. This forces a decisive win of material, as White's Queen cannot guard the Rook if it retreats.

Puzzle No. 19 With proper play White can set up a winning skewer attack. He starts with 1 R—R6 ch, forcing the Black King to its fourth rank. White then continues with 2 R—R5 ch—a skewer attack that wins the Black Rook.

Puzzle No. 20 White plays 1 Q—R5 ch, forcing 1.., K × P. White then follows up with 2 Q—R4 ch, skewering the Black King and Queen.

Puzzle No. 21 The immediate skewer with 1 Q—B3 ch ? ? is of course impossible because of 1 . ., K×Q.

White therefore needs a preliminary move: 1 N—Q6 ch forcing 1 . ., K—Q4. Then 2 Q—B3 ch neatly skewers the Black King and Queen.

Puzzle No. 22 White forces the opening of the Queen file with 1 N×P ch forking the Black King and Queen. Then, after 1 . ., P×N, White skewers the Black King and Queen with 2 Q—Q8 ch.

Puzzle No. 23 It is not necessary for Black to defend his Pawn, as R×P can always be answered by . ., R—R7 ch, a skewer attack on the White King and Rook. Black's strongest move is therefore 1 . ., R—R8! threatening to queen the Pawn.

White is helpless against this threat, for after 2 R×P his King and Rook will be skewered by Black's Rook (2 . ., R—R7 ch etc.).

Puzzle No. 24 White has a beautiful winning resource in 1 Q—N1 ch! After 1 . ., Q×Q the pin is relieved and White can play 2 P—N8/Q ch skewering Black's King and Queen. Note that White can also promote to a Rook with the same effect. But of course the subsequent mate with the Queen is quicker.

Puzzle No. 25 White forks the Black King and Rook with 1 Q—Q5 ch. Black must get his King out of check and has no time to save his Rook.

Puzzle No. 26 With 1 B×P ch White forks the Black King and Queen Rook. With his King in check, Black has no time to save his menaced Rook.

Puzzle No. 27 White attacks one of the Black Rooks with 1 P—KN4. This is decisive, for after the attacked Rook moves away, White continues 2 P—N5 ch, forking the Black King and the other Rook.

Puzzle No. 28 Black has a false try with 1 . ., P—Q4, a Pawn fork that *seems* to win a piece. But White escapes with 2 N×N CHECK. So Black must look for a different method. Here it is:

1	N×N
2 Q×N	P—Q4

Now the Pawn fork works perfectly: Black wins a piece.

Puzzle No. 29 White's winning move is 1 K—B3. This leaves the attacked Bishop a choice of four possible squares to avoid immediate capture.

Here are the consequences of these four moves:

If Black plays either 1.., B—R5 or 1.., B—R7 White replies 2 R—QR6 ch.

If Black plays 1.., B—N1 White replies 2 R—Q8 ch.

If Black plays 1.., B—B2 White replies 2 R—Q8 ch. Now Black's King must move up to the second rank, whereupon White continues 3 R—Q7 ch.

In every one of these instances White's Rook forks the Black King and Bishop.

Puzzle No. 30 With 1 N×B White sets up the position for a Queen fork of the Black King and the remaining Black Bishop.

Black must reply 1.., P×N to regain his lost material, allowing White's 2 Q—R5 ch forking King and Bishop.

Puzzle No. 31 White aims for Q—K4 forking Black's King Rook Pawn and his Queen Rook. But first he must remove Black's protective Knight. Therefore:

　　　　　1 B×N　　　　　　　　B×B

Or 1.., P×B; 2 Q—K4 with the same effect.

　　　　　2 Q—K4 and wins

White's Queen fork threatens 3 Q×RP mate or 3 Q×R. Black must stop mate and therefore he cannot save the menaced Rook.

Puzzle No. 32 White smashes up the Black position with 1 R×P! Then, after Black's reply 1.., R×R White continues 2 B×P ch, forking the Black King and Rook.

Puzzle No. 33 The strongest discovered check is 1 N×B dis ch, as the White Knight captures the Black Bishop free of charge.

In reply to this capture Black of course has no time for 1.., P×N, as his King is in check. He would therefore have to play 1.., K—R1 to get out of check. This would give White time to move his Knight to safety—2 N—B6, for example, would be excellent.

The upshot, then, is that 1 N×B dis ch wins a piece for White.

Puzzle No. 34 By far the strongest discovered check available to White is 1 N—B6 dis ch.

This powerful move wins Black's Queen. As Black must get out of check, he has no time to save his Queen. Of course 1.., Q—K2 is of no avail, as White still has 2 N × Q.

Puzzle No. 35 The right move for Black is 1.., R—KB7 dis ch! Black parries White's check and simultaneously gives check himself, as well as attacking the White Queen, which is thus lost.

Puzzle No. 36 Black sets up a discovered check with the astounding move 1.., Q—Q8 ch! This forces White's Queen away from the blockade with these consequences:

2 Q × Q	P—K7 dis ch

The discovered check is ruinous for White. For example, if he plays 3 K—R1, Black captures the White Queen, promoting to a new Queen himself and checkmating next move. The other possibility is:

3 Q—Q4	P—K8/Q ch

Black can also force checkmate by 3.., B × Q ch etc.

4 B—B1	B × Q ch
5 K—R1	Q × B mate

Note that 1.., Q—Q7 ?? would have been a horrible blunder because of 2 Q—R5 mate.

Puzzle No. 37 The strongest double check is 1.., N—B6 dbl ch, for after 2 K—R1 (forced) Black replies 2.., Q × RP mate.

The other double check forces checkmate too but takes a move longer. For after 1.., N—K7 dbl ch White must still play 2 K—R1. Then comes 2.., N—N6 ch! forcing 3 P × N, after which 3.., Q—R4 mate.

Puzzle No. 38 White begins with 1 R—N7 ch, which gives him a whole series of discovered checks:

1	K—R1
2 R × B dis ch	K—N1

Now White continues to win more and more material.

3 R—N7 ch	K—R1
4 R × P dis ch	K—N1

5 R—N7 ch	K—R1
6 R×P dis ch	K—N1
7 R—N7 ch	K—R1
8 R×P dis ch	K—N1
9 R×R and wins	

With a whole Rook ahead, White naturally has a very easy win. Because of the amusing back-and-forth movements of the Rook, such a sequence of discovered checks is called a "mill".

Puzzle No. 39 White's winning move is 1 R—N3 ch!

If Black refuses the Rook, White simply continues 2 R × R winning easily.

However, if Black replies 1.., K × R White continues 2 P—B8/ Q dis ch. Black cannot capture the new Queen because he is in check. After Black gets out of check White follows up with 3 Q × R with an overwhelming material advantage.

Puzzle No. 40 White's astounding first move, relying on the coming discovered check, is 1 Q × NP ch!!

Then, after the forced reply 1.., K × Q White replies 2 B × R dis ch, winning the Rook and then the Queen and coming out two pieces ahead with a very easy win.

Puzzle No. 41 Black plays 1.., Q × Q, removing one of the White Bishop's defenders. Then, after 2 P × Q, Black captures the Bishop, with a piece to the good.

Puzzle No. 42 White wins a piece with 1 Q × B!

This capture is made possible by the vulnerable state of Black's back row; for if he stops to capture the Queen, White forces checkmate with 2 R—K8 ch, R × R; 3 R × R mate.

Puzzle No. 43 Black can force checkmate in four moves, beginning with the removal of White's vitally important defensive Bishop:

1	R × B ch!
2 K × R	Q × P ch
3 K—K1	N—Q6 ch
4 K—Q1	B—B6 mate

Puzzle No. 44 White deflects the Black Rook with 1 R—B2 ch! for after 1.., R×R White can queen his Pawn.

The resulting ending of Queen against Rook is fairly easy to win as Black's King has comparatively little mobility.

Puzzle No. 45 Black's King has to protect the Black Queen. By playing 1 B×P ch! White deflects the Black King 1.., K×B can be answered 2 Q×Q and White wins.

Puzzle No. 46 Instead of losing his Queen, White forces checkmate in this manner:

1 R—KB1 ch	K—N1
2 R—B8 ch!	....

This clever resource deflects the Black Rook from the King file.

2	R×R
3 Q—N7 mate	

Puzzle No. 47 White's Knight is overworked as it has to guard both the White Rook and Knight.

Black exploits the situation by playing 1.., R×R ch. After 2 N×R there follows 2.., B×B leaving Black a piece to the good with an easy win.

Puzzle No. 48 Black's Rook is overworked because of its double defensive task.

White proves this by playing 1 B×P ch. This forces 1.., R×B allowing White to continue 2 Q×Q ch with an easy win.

Puzzle No. 49 Black's Bishop must prevent White's Queen Knight Pawn from queening. Black's King must guard the Bishop. Here is how White reduces the Black pieces to an overworked state:

1 P—N5 ch	K—B4

Obviously Black's only reasonable move.

2 P—N6	....

Now White threatens to win with 3 P—N7 for the overworked Bishop would then be unable to hold back both Pawns.

2	K—B3
3 P—N7	....

Black's King is now overworked, having the double task of guarding the Bishop and preventing the King Knight Pawn from queening.

    3 ....   K×P

    4 K×B and wins

Black is helpless against the queening of the remaining White Pawn.

Puzzle No. 50 White mates in this fashion:

    1 R—QN2 ch   K moves

    2 R—QR3 mate

Puzzle No. 51 Black starts with 1.., R—KR1! This leaves White with only one move: 2 K—B1, allowing Black to carry out his plan with 2.., R—R8 mate.

Puzzle No. 52 By sacrificing his Queen, Black forces a quick mate. After 1.., Q—Q8 ch! White must play 2 R×Q, whereupon 2.., R×R mate follows.

Puzzle No. 53 White achieves his end with 1 B—K6 ch, K—R1; 2 R—B8 mate.

On the other hand, if Black had moved first, he would have checkmated in this way:

    1 ....   R×P ch

    2 K—R1   R×P ch

    3 K—N1   R/N7—N7 mate

Puzzle No. 54 Black plays 1.., R—R8 ch. White must capture the Rook, allowing 2.., R×R mate. White's King has no flight square because of the Black Pawn wedge at King Knight 6.

Puzzle No. 55 White's Queen is far away and White's pieces are undeveloped. Hence Black can carry out a concentrated onslaught:

    1 ....   N—K7 ch

    2 K—R1   Q×P ch!

    3 K×Q   R—KR5 mate

Puzzle No. 56 Here we have a very similar situation. White is in no position to put up a satisfactory defence, so Black triumphs with:

1	N—N6 ch!
2 P×N	Q—R4 mate

Puzzle No. 57 The overworked status of the Black Queen is the key to the situation:

1 R—K8 ch!	B—B1

If Black captures the Rook, White replies 2 Q—N5 mate.

2 Q—N5 ch	Q×Q
3 R×B mate	

White can also checkmate by starting with 1 Q—N5 ch etc.

Puzzle No. 58 No, Black must not play 1.., K×R?? because of the reply 2 B×P mate.

Puzzle No. 59 White's Bishop delivers a typical checkmate:

1 R—KN3 ch	K—R1
2 B×P mate	

Puzzle No. 60 It would be a mistake on White's part to begin with 1 B—R6 ch, for then Black's King would escape with 1.., K—K2, considerably lengthening the mating process. The right way is:

1 B—B5 ch	K—N1
2 B—Q5 ch	K—R1
3 B—Q4 mate	

Puzzle No. 61 White's winning move is 1 R—K8 ch! Black then has the sorry choice between 1.., Q×R; 2 B×B mate, or 1.., K—N2; 2 R×Q, and after 2.., B×B White has a very easy win.

Puzzle No. 62 White forces mate in two moves:

1 R×N ch!	P×R
2 B×P mate	

A splendid example of the power of the two Bishops.

Puzzle No. 63 White has an amazing first move:

1 Q—R6 ch!	K×Q
2 B×R mate	

Puzzle No. 64 Here Black has a somewhat similar mate, beginning with an equally remarkable sacrifice:

1		Q×P ch!
2 N×Q		N—N6 ch
3 K—N1		B—B4 ch
4 R—K3		B×R mate

Puzzle No. 65 Once more the mating process starts with a Queen sacrifice:

1 Q×P ch!		R×Q

If Black moves his King, there follows 2 Q—N7 mate or 2 Q—R8 mate.

2 B×R ch		K—N1
3 B×P mate		

Puzzle No. 66 White plays 1 Q—R7! forcing Black to reply 1.., K—Q1. Then comes 2 Q—N8 mate or 2 Q—Q7 mate.

Note, however, that 1 Q—N6 (which looks equally powerful) would be a terrible blunder, as it would stalemate Black.

Puzzle No. 67 White mates in the following manner:

1 B×P ch		K—R1
2 B—N6 dis ch		....

This important move shuts off the Black Queen and makes the mate possible on the fourth move.

2		K—N1
3 Q—R7 ch		K—B1
4 Q×P mate		

Puzzle No. 68 The important move for White is 1 Q—KN4!, preventing Black's King from fleeing to King Knight 8. Then, after the forced reply 1.., K—K8, White can continue 2 Q—Q1 mate.

Puzzle No. 69 White engineers a back-row mate with:

1 R×N ch		K×R
2 Q—Q8 mate		

Puzzle No. 70 White sacrifices with 1 R×P ch! This forces 1.., P×R, permitting 2 Q—B7 mate.

Puzzle No. 71 As we have seen, 1 Q—R7 ch doesn't work. The right way is:

1	R—R8 ch!	K × R
2	Q—R7 mate	

Puzzle No. 72 White's Bishop must move, but where? The right way is:

1	B—N6 ch!	P × B
2	Q—K7 mate	

Note that 1 B—N5 ch?—apparently with the same effect—is met by 1 . ., P × B dis ch!

Puzzle No. 73 If it is White's move he forces mate in this way:

1	R—R8 ch	K × R
2	Q—R5 ch	....

Of course 2 Q—R4 ch or 2 Q—R3 ch also does the trick.

2	....	K—N1
3	Q—R7 mate	

If Black moves first, he too has a mating attack:

1	....	R—B8 ch
2	K—R2	R—KR8 ch!
3	K × R	Q × RP ch
4	K—N1	Q—N7 mate

Puzzle No. 74 White must deflect the Black Queen:

1	Q × P ch!	Q × Q
2	N—B7 mate	

Puzzle No. 75 The sacrifice of the Black Queen is the prelude to a neat checkmate:

1	....	Q—N7 ch!
2	R × Q	N—R6 mate

Puzzle No. 76 White starts with a waiting move which forces Black to trap his own King:

1	N—B1	P—R7

Now the Black King has no flight square.

2	N—N3 mate	

Puzzle No. 77 Black must put the White Rook at King Bishop 1 out of action:

1	R—N8 ch!
2 R×R	N—B7 mate

Puzzle No. 78 A Rook sacrifice exposes White's King to a fatal attack:

1	R×P ch!
2 P×R	N—N6 mate

Puzzle No. 79 To achieve checkmate, White's Knight belongs at King Rook 6:

1 R—N6 ch!	P×R
2 N—R6 mate	

Puzzle No. 80 White plays 1 N—Q5! threatening 2 N×P mate and also 2 Q×Q. Black can stop this mate only at the cost of parting with his unprotected Queen.

Puzzle No. 81 Black wins with the astounding move 1.., N—N5! threatening 2.., Q×P mate.

The main point is that on 2 Q×Q Black has the pretty reply 2.., N—B7 mate.

White can parry the mate threat—but only at the cost of ruinous loss of material—with such moves as 2 R×N (allowing 2.., Q×Q ch) or 2 R—N2 (allowing 2.., P×R ch etc.).

A PERSONAL WORD FROM MELVIN POWERS
PUBLISHER, WILSHIRE BOOK COMPANY

Dear Friend:

My goal is to publish interesting, informative, and inspirational books. You can help me accomplish this by answering the following questions, either by phone or by mail. Or, if convenient for you, I would welcome the opportunity to visit with you in my office and hear your comments in person.

Did you enjoy reading this book? Why?

Would you enjoy reading another similar book?

What idea in the book impressed you the most?

If applicable to your situation, have you incorporated this idea in your daily life?

Is there a chapter that could serve as a theme for an entire book? Please explain.

If you have an idea for a book, I would welcome discussing it with you. If you already have one in progress, write or call me concerning possible publication. I can be reached at (213) 875-1711 or (818) 983-1105.

Sincerely yours,

MELVIN POWERS

12015 Sherman Road
North Hollywood, California 91605

MELVIN POWERS SELF-IMPROVEMENT LIBRARY

ASTROLOGY
_____ ASTROLOGY: HOW TO CHART YOUR HOROSCOPE *Max Heindel*   5.00
_____ ASTROLOGY AND SEXUAL ANALYSIS *Morris C. Goodman*   5.00
_____ ASTROLOGY MADE EASY *Astarte*   3.00
_____ ASTROLOGY MADE PRACTICAL *Alexandra Kayhle*   3.00
_____ ASTROLOGY, ROMANCE, YOU AND THE STARS *Anthony Norvell*   5.00
_____ MY WORLD OF ASTROLOGY *Sydney Omarr*   7.00
_____ THOUGHT DIAL *Sydney Omarr*   4.00
_____ WHAT THE STARS REVEAL ABOUT THE MEN IN YOUR LIFE *Thelma White*   3.00

BRIDGE
_____ BRIDGE BIDDING MADE EASY *Edwin B. Kantar*   10.00
_____ BRIDGE CONVENTIONS *Edwin B. Kantar*   7.00
_____ BRIDGE HUMOR *Edwin B. Kantar*   5.00
_____ COMPETITIVE BIDDING IN MODERN BRIDGE *Edgar Kaplan*   7.00
_____ DEFENSIVE BRIDGE PLAY COMPLETE *Edwin B. Kantar*   15.00
_____ GAMESMAN BRIDGE — Play Better with Kantar *Edwin B. Kantar*   5.00
_____ HOW TO IMPROVE YOUR BRIDGE *Alfred Sheinwold*   5.00
_____ IMPROVING YOUR BIDDING SKILLS *Edwin B. Kantar*   4.00
_____ INTRODUCTION TO DECLARER'S PLAY *Edwin B. Kantar*   5.00
_____ INTRODUCTION TO DEFENDER'S PLAY *Edwin B. Kantar*   3.00
_____ KANTAR FOR THE DEFENSE *Edwin B. Kantar*   7.00
_____ KANTAR FOR THE DEFENSE VOLUME 2 *Edwin B. Kantar*   7.00
_____ SHORT CUT TO WINNING BRIDGE *Alfred Sheinwold*   3.00
_____ TEST YOUR BRIDGE PLAY *Edwin B. Kantar*   5.00
_____ VOLUME 2 — TEST YOUR BRIDGE PLAY *Edwin B. Kantar*   5.00
_____ WINNING DECLARER PLAY *Dorothy Hayden Truscott*   5.00

BUSINESS, STUDY & REFERENCE
_____ CONVERSATION MADE EASY *Elliot Russell*   4.00
_____ EXAM SECRET *Dennis B. Jackson*   3.00
_____ FIX-IT BOOK *Arthur Symons*   2.00
_____ HOW TO DEVELOP A BETTER SPEAKING VOICE *M. Hellier*   4.00
_____ HOW TO SELF-PUBLISH YOUR BOOK & MAKE IT A BEST SELLER *Melvin Powers*   10.00
_____ INCREASE YOUR LEARNING POWER *Geoffrey A. Dudley*   3.00
_____ PRACTICAL GUIDE TO BETTER CONCENTRATION *Melvin Powers*   3.00
_____ PRACTICAL GUIDE TO PUBLIC SPEAKING *Maurice Forley*   5.00
_____ 7 DAYS TO FASTER READING *William S. Schaill*   3.00
_____ SONGWRITERS' RHYMING DICTIONARY *Jane Shaw Whitfield*   7.00
_____ SPELLING MADE EASY *Lester D. Basch & Dr. Milton Finkelstein*   3.00
_____ STUDENT'S GUIDE TO BETTER GRADES *J. A. Rickard*   3.00
_____ TEST YOURSELF — Find Your Hidden Talent *Jack Shafer*   3.00
_____ YOUR WILL & WHAT TO DO ABOUT IT *Attorney Samuel G. Kling*   5.00

CALLIGRAPHY
_____ ADVANCED CALLIGRAPHY *Katherine Jeffares*   7.00
_____ CALLIGRAPHER'S REFERENCE BOOK *Anne Leptich & Jacque Evans*   7.00
_____ CALLIGRAPHY — The Art of Beautiful Writing *Katherine Jeffares*   7.00
_____ CALLIGRAPHY FOR FUN & PROFIT *Anne Leptich & Jacque Evans*   7.00
_____ CALLIGRAPHY MADE EASY *Tina Serafini*   7.00

CHESS & CHECKERS
_____ BEGINNER'S GUIDE TO WINNING CHESS *Fred Reinfeld*   5.00
_____ CHESS IN TEN EASY LESSONS *Larry Evans*   5.00
_____ CHESS MADE EASY *Milton L. Hanauer*   3.00
_____ CHESS PROBLEMS FOR BEGINNERS *edited by Fred Reinfeld*   2.00
_____ CHESS SECRETS REVEALED *Fred Reinfeld*   2.00
_____ CHESS TACTICS FOR BEGINNERS *edited by Fred Reinfeld*   5.00
_____ CHESS THEORY & PRACTICE *Morry & Mitchell*   2.00
_____ HOW TO WIN AT CHECKERS *Fred Reinfeld*   3.00
_____ 1001 BRILLIANT WAYS TO CHECKMATE *Fred Reinfeld*   5.00
_____ 1001 WINNING CHESS SACRIFICES & COMBINATIONS *Fred Reinfeld*   5.00
_____ SOVIET CHESS *Edited by R. G. Wade*   3.00

COOKERY & HERBS

_____ CULPEPER'S HERBAL REMEDIES *Dr. Nicholas Culpeper* — 3.00
_____ FAST GOURMET COOKBOOK *Poppy Cannon* — 2.50
_____ GINSENG The Myth & The Truth *Joseph P. Hou* — 3.00
_____ HEALING POWER OF HERBS *May Bethel* — 4.00
_____ HEALING POWER OF NATURAL FOODS *May Bethel* — 5.00
_____ HERB HANDBOOK *Dawn MacLeod* — 3.00
_____ HERBS FOR HEALTH — How to Grow & Use Them *Louise Evans Doole* — 4.00
_____ HOME GARDEN COOKBOOK — Delicious Natural Food Recipes *Ken Kraft* — 3.00
_____ MEDICAL HERBALIST *edited by Dr. J. R. Yemm* — 3.00
_____ VEGETABLE GARDENING FOR BEGINNERS *Hugh Wiberg* — 2.00
_____ VEGETABLES FOR TODAY'S GARDENS *R. Milton Carleton* — 2.00
_____ VEGETARIAN COOKERY *Janet Walker* — 4.00
_____ VEGETARIAN COOKING MADE EASY & DELECTABLE *Veronica Vezza* — 3.00
_____ VEGETARIAN DELIGHTS — A Happy Cookbook for Health *K. R. Mehta* — 2.00
_____ VEGETARIAN GOURMET COOKBOOK *Joyce McKinnel* — 3.00

GAMBLING & POKER

_____ ADVANCED POKER STRATEGY & WINNING PLAY *A. D. Livingston* — 5.00
_____ HOW TO WIN AT DICE GAMES *Skip Frey* — 3.00
_____ HOW TO WIN AT POKER *Terence Reese & Anthony T. Watkins* — 5.00
_____ WINNING AT CRAPS *Dr. Lloyd T. Commins* — 4.00
_____ WINNING AT GIN *Chester Wander & Cy Rice* — 3.00
_____ WINNING AT POKER — An Expert's Guide *John Archer* — 5.00
_____ WINNING AT 21 — An Expert's Guide *John Archer* — 5.00
_____ WINNING POKER SYSTEMS *Norman Zadeh* — 3.00

HEALTH

_____ BEE POLLEN *Lynda Lyngheim & Jack Scagnetti* — 3.00
_____ DR. LINDNER'S SPECIAL WEIGHT CONTROL METHOD *P. G. Lindner, M.D.* — 2.00
_____ HELP YOURSELF TO BETTER SIGHT *Margaret Darst Corbett* — 3.00
_____ HOW TO IMPROVE YOUR VISION *Dr. Robert A. Kraskin* — 3.00
_____ HOW YOU CAN STOP SMOKING PERMANENTLY *Ernest Caldwell* — 3.00
_____ MIND OVER PLATTER *Peter G. Lindner, M.D.* — 3.00
_____ NATURE'S WAY TO NUTRITION & VIBRANT HEALTH *Robert J. Scrutton* — 3.00
_____ NEW CARBOHYDRATE DIET COUNTER *Patti Lopez-Pereira* — 2.00
_____ QUICK & EASY EXERCISES FOR FACIAL BEAUTY *Judy Smith-deal* — 2.00
_____ QUICK & EASY EXERCISES FOR FIGURE BEAUTY *Judy Smith-deal* — 2.00
_____ REFLEXOLOGY *Dr. Maybelle Segal* — 4.00
_____ REFLEXOLOGY FOR GOOD HEALTH *Anna Kaye & Don C. Matchan* — 5.00
_____ 30 DAYS TO BEAUTIFUL LEGS *Dr. Marc Selner* — 3.00
_____ YOU CAN LEARN TO RELAX *Dr. Samuel Gutwirth* — 3.00
_____ YOUR ALLERGY — What To Do About It *Allan Knight, M.D.* — 3.00

HOBBIES

_____ BEACHCOMBING FOR BEGINNERS *Norman Hickin* — 2.00
_____ BLACKSTONE'S MODERN CARD TRICKS *Harry Blackstone* — 3.00
_____ BLACKSTONE'S SECRETS OF MAGIC *Harry Blackstone* — 3.00
_____ COIN COLLECTING FOR BEGINNERS *Burton Hobson & Fred Reinfeld* — 5.00
_____ ENTERTAINING WITH ESP *Tony 'Doc' Shiels* — 2.00
_____ 400 FASCINATING MAGIC TRICKS YOU CAN DO *Howard Thurston* — 4.00
_____ HOW I TURN JUNK INTO FUN AND PROFIT *Sari* — 3.00
_____ HOW TO WRITE A HIT SONG & SELL IT *Tommy Boyce* — 7.00
_____ JUGGLING MADE EASY *Rudolf Dittrich* — 3.00
_____ MAGIC FOR ALL AGES *Walter Gibson* — 4.00
_____ MAGIC MADE EASY *Byron Wels* — 2.00
_____ STAMP COLLECTING FOR BEGINNERS *Burton Hobson* — 3.00

HORSE PLAYERS' WINNING GUIDES

_____ BETTING HORSES TO WIN *Les Conklin* — 5.00
_____ ELIMINATE THE LOSERS *Bob McKnight* — 3.00
_____ HOW TO PICK WINNING HORSES *Bob McKnight* — 5.00
_____ HOW TO WIN AT THE RACES *Sam (The Genius) Lewin* — 5.00
_____ HOW YOU CAN BEAT THE RACES *Jack Kavanagh* — 5.00
_____ MAKING MONEY AT THE RACES *David Barr* — 5.00

____ PAYDAY AT THE RACES *Les Conklin*	5.00
____ SMART HANDICAPPING MADE EASY *William Bauman*	5.00
____ SUCCESS AT THE HARNESS RACES *Barry Meadow*	5.00
____ WINNING AT THE HARNESS RACES — An Expert's Guide *Nick Cammarano*	5.00

HUMOR

____ HOW TO FLATTEN YOUR TUSH *Coach Marge Reardon*	2.00
____ HOW TO MAKE LOVE TO YOURSELF *Ron Stevens & Joy Grdnic*	3.00
____ JOKE TELLER'S HANDBOOK *Bob Orben*	5.00
____ JOKES FOR ALL OCCASIONS *Al Schock*	5.00
____ 2000 NEW LAUGHS FOR SPEAKERS *Bob Orben*	5.00
____ 2,500 JOKES TO START 'EM LAUGHING *Bob Orben*	5.00

HYPNOTISM

____ ADVANCED TECHNIQUES OF HYPNOSIS *Melvin Powers*	3.00
____ BRAINWASHING AND THE CULTS *Paul A. Verdier, Ph.D.*	3.00
____ CHILDBIRTH WITH HYPNOSIS *William S. Kroger, M.D.*	5.00
____ HOW TO SOLVE Your Sex Problems with Self-Hypnosis *Frank S. Caprio, M.D.*	5.00
____ HOW TO STOP SMOKING THRU SELF-HYPNOSIS *Leslie M. LeCron*	3.00
____ HOW TO USE AUTO-SUGGESTION EFFECTIVELY *John Duckworth*	3.00
____ HOW YOU CAN BOWL BETTER USING SELF-HYPNOSIS *Jack Heise*	4.00
____ HOW YOU CAN PLAY BETTER GOLF USING SELF-HYPNOSIS *Jack Heise*	3.00
____ HYPNOSIS AND SELF-HYPNOSIS *Bernard Hollander, M.D.*	5.00
____ HYPNOTISM *(Originally published in 1893) Carl Sextus*	5.00
____ HYPNOTISM & PSYCHIC PHENOMENA *Simeon Edmunds*	4.00
____ HYPNOTISM MADE EASY *Dr. Ralph Winn*	3.00
____ HYPNOTISM MADE PRACTICAL *Louis Orton*	5.00
____ HYPNOTISM REVEALED *Melvin Powers*	3.00
____ HYPNOTISM TODAY *Leslie LeCron and Jean Bordeaux, Ph.D.*	5.00
____ MODERN HYPNOSIS *Lesley Kuhn & Salvatore Russo, Ph.D.*	5.00
____ NEW CONCEPTS OF HYPNOSIS *Bernard C. Gindes, M.D.*	7.00
____ NEW SELF-HYPNOSIS *Paul Adams*	5.00
____ POST-HYPNOTIC INSTRUCTIONS — Suggestions for Therapy *Arnold Furst*	5.00
____ PRACTICAL GUIDE TO SELF-HYPNOSIS *Melvin Powers*	3.00
____ PRACTICAL HYPNOTISM *Philip Magonet, M.D.*	3.00
____ SECRETS OF HYPNOTISM *S. J. Van Pelt, M.D.*	5.00
____ SELF-HYPNOSIS A Conditioned-Response Technique *Laurence Sparks*	7.00
____ SELF-HYPNOSIS Its Theory, Technique & Application *Melvin Powers*	3.00
____ THERAPY THROUGH HYPNOSIS *edited by Raphael H. Rhodes*	5.00

JUDAICA

____ MODERN ISRAEL *Lily Edelman*	2.00
____ SERVICE OF THE HEART *Evelyn Garfiel, Ph.D.*	7.00
____ STORY OF ISRAEL IN COINS *Jean & Maurice Gould*	2.00
____ STORY OF ISRAEL IN STAMPS *Maxim & Gabriel Shamir*	1.00
____ TONGUE OF THE PROPHETS *Robert St. John*	7.00

JUST FOR WOMEN

____ COSMOPOLITAN'S GUIDE TO MARVELOUS MEN Fwd. by *Helen Gurley Brown*	3.00
____ COSMOPOLITAN'S HANG-UP HANDBOOK Foreword by *Helen Gurley Brown*	4.00
____ COSMOPOLITAN'S LOVE BOOK — A Guide to Ecstasy in Bed	5.00
____ COSMOPOLITAN'S NEW ETIQUETTE GUIDE Fwd. by *Helen Gurley Brown*	4.00
____ I AM A COMPLEAT WOMAN *Doris Hagopian & Karen O'Connor Sweeney*	3.00
____ JUST FOR WOMEN — A Guide to the Female Body *Richard E. Sand, M.D.*	5.00
____ NEW APPROACHES TO SEX IN MARRIAGE *John E. Eichenlaub, M.D.*	3.00
____ SEXUALLY ADEQUATE FEMALE *Frank S. Caprio, M.D.*	3.00
____ SEXUALLY FULFILLED WOMAN *Dr. Rachel Copelan*	5.00
____ YOUR FIRST YEAR OF MARRIAGE *Dr. Tom McGinnis*	3.00

MARRIAGE, SEX & PARENTHOOD

____ ABILITY TO LOVE *Dr. Allan Fromme*	6.00
____ GUIDE TO SUCCESSFUL MARRIAGE *Drs. Albert Ellis & Robert Harper*	5.00
____ HOW TO RAISE AN EMOTIONALLY HEALTHY, HAPPY CHILD *A. Ellis*	5.00
____ SEX WITHOUT GUILT *Albert Ellis, Ph.D.*	5.00
____ SEXUALLY ADEQUATE MALE *Frank S. Caprio, M.D.*	3.00

_____ NEVER UNDERESTIMATE THE SELLING POWER OF A WOMAN _Dottie Walters_	7.00
_____ NEW GUIDE TO RATIONAL LIVING _Albert Ellis, Ph.D. & R. Harper, Ph.D._	3.00
_____ PROJECT YOU _A Manual of Rational Assertiveness Training Paris & Casey_	6.00
_____ PSYCHO-CYBERNETICS _Maxwell Maltz, M.D._	5.00
_____ PSYCHOLOGY OF HANDWRITING _Nadya Olyanova_	7.00
_____ SALES CYBERNETICS _Brian Adams_	7.00
_____ SCIENCE OF MIND IN DAILY LIVING _Dr. Donald Curtis_	5.00
_____ SECRET OF SECRETS _U. S. Andersen_	7.00
_____ SECRET POWER OF THE PYRAMIDS _U. S. Andersen_	7.00
_____ SELF-THERAPY FOR THE STUTTERER _Malcolm Frazer_	3.00
_____ STUTTERING AND WHAT YOU CAN DO ABOUT IT _W. Johnson, Ph.D._	2.50
_____ SUCCESS-CYBERNETICS _U. S. Andersen_	6.00
_____ 10 DAYS TO A GREAT NEW LIFE _William E. Edwards_	3.00
_____ THINK AND GROW RICH _Napoleon Hill_	5.00
_____ THINK YOUR WAY TO SUCCESS _Dr. Lew Losoncy_	5.00
_____ THREE MAGIC WORDS _U. S. Andersen_	7.00
_____ TREASURY OF COMFORT _edited by Rabbi Sidney Greenberg_	5.00
_____ TREASURY OF THE ART OF LIVING _Sidney S. Greenberg_	5.00
_____ WHAT YOUR HANDWRITING REVEALS _Albert E. Hughes_	3.00
_____ YOU ARE NOT THE TARGET _Laura Huxley_	5.00
_____ YOUR SUBCONSCIOUS POWER _Charles M. Simmons_	5.00
_____ YOUR THOUGHTS CAN CHANGE YOUR LIFE _Dr. Donald Curtis_	5.00

SPORTS

_____ BICYCLING FOR FUN AND GOOD HEALTH _Kenneth E. Luther_	2.00
_____ BILLIARDS — Pocket • Carom • Three Cushion _Clive Cottingham, Jr._	5.00
_____ CAMPING-OUT 101 Ideas & Activities _Bruno Knobel_	2.00
_____ COMPLETE GUIDE TO FISHING _Vlad Evanoff_	2.00
_____ HOW TO IMPROVE YOUR RACQUETBALL _Lubarsky Kaufman & Scagnetti_	3.00
_____ HOW TO WIN AT POCKET BILLIARDS _Edward D. Knuchell_	5.00
_____ JOY OF WALKING _Jack Scagnetti_	3.00
_____ LEARNING & TEACHING SOCCER SKILLS _Eric Worthington_	3.00
_____ MOTORCYCLING FOR BEGINNERS _I. G. Edmonds_	3.00
_____ RACQUETBALL FOR WOMEN _Toni Hudson, Jack Scagnetti & Vince Rondone_	3.00
_____ RACQUETBALL MADE EASY _Steve Lubarsky, Rod Delson & Jack Scagnetti_	5.00
_____ SECRET OF BOWLING STRIKES _Dawson Taylor_	5.00
_____ SECRET OF PERFECT PUTTING _Horton Smith & Dawson Taylor_	5.00
_____ SOCCER — The Game & How to Play It _Gary Rosenthal_	5.00
_____ STARTING SOCCER _Edward F. Dolan, Jr._	3.00

TENNIS LOVERS' LIBRARY

_____ BEGINNER'S GUIDE TO WINNING TENNIS _Helen Hull Jacobs_	2.00
_____ HOW TO BEAT BETTER TENNIS PLAYERS _Loring Fiske_	4.00
_____ HOW TO IMPROVE YOUR TENNIS — Style, Strategy & Analysis _C. Wilson_	2.00
_____ PLAY TENNIS WITH ROSEWALL _Ken Rosewall_	2.00
_____ PSYCH YOURSELF TO BETTER TENNIS _Dr. Walter A. Luszki_	2.00
_____ TENNIS FOR BEGINNERS, _Dr. H. A. Murray_	2.00
_____ TENNIS MADE EASY _Joel Brecheen_	4.00
_____ WEEKEND TENNIS — How to Have Fun & Win at the Same Time _Bill Talbert_	3.00
_____ WINNING WITH PERCENTAGE TENNIS — Smart Strategy _Jack Lowe_	2.00

WILSHIRE PET LIBRARY

_____ DOG OBEDIENCE TRAINING _Gust Kessopulos_	5.00
_____ DOG TRAINING MADE EASY & FUN _John W. Kellogg_	4.00
_____ HOW TO BRING UP YOUR PET DOG _Kurt Unkelbach_	2.00
_____ HOW TO RAISE & TRAIN YOUR PUPPY _Jeff Griffen_	5.00
_____ PIGEONS: HOW TO RAISE & TRAIN THEM _William H. Allen, Jr._	2.00

_The books listed above can be obtained from your book dealer or directly from
Melvin Powers. When ordering, please remit $1.00 postage for the first book
and 50¢ for each additional book._

Melvin Powers
12015 Sherman Road, No. Hollywood, California 91605

Notes

Notes

Notes

Notes

Notes

Notes

Notes

SHORT GAMES

P. 85 (2)

107

PUZZLE 30 ?

PUZZLE 65 MATE IN 4
(I FOUND A MATE IN 5
W/ NO SACRIFISE

My Puppy

Story by Joy Cowley

"My puppy."

"No! My puppy."

"No!

My puppy!"

"No! My puppy."

"No!"

"My puppy!"